Flower visualization is a form of meditation that involves focusing on a particular flower, either in your mind's eye or by physically looking at the flower, to promote relaxation, calmness, and overall well-being. To practice flower visualization, one can start by selecting a flower that resonates with them or simply choosing a flower that is readily available. Then, sit in a comfortable position, close your eyes or look at the flower, and focus on its beauty and details. You can visualize the colors, textures, and shapes of the flower, and imagine the scent and the feeling of the flower. As you focus on the flower, you can take slow and deep breaths, allowing your body to relax and your mind to become calm. You can also repeat positive affirmations or mantras to further enhance the relaxation and positive energy. Flower visualization has been used as a form of meditation and relaxation for centuries and is believed to promote feelings of peace, harmony, and connection with nature. It can be practiced by anyone, regardless of their meditation experience, and can be easily incorporated into a daily routine.